IN
PURSUIT
OF
God

A 100-DAY
DEVOTIONAL

EDDIE JAMES

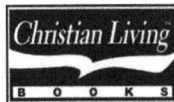

Largo, MD

ISBN 9781562293994

Christian Living Books, Inc.
P.O. Box 7584
Largo, MD 20792
christianlivingbooks.com
We bring your dreams to fruition.

INTRODUCTION

In this ever-demanding world, life can be so over-whelming that we lose our way. The pressures we face from day-to-day can negatively impact our emotional, physical, and mental well-being. Sometimes, our relationships with God and others hit rock bottom, and we don't know where to turn. Life's storms, our culture, and people's opinions cause us to doubt, instill fear, and lose faith. We need divine wisdom to rise from the abyss of chaos and confusion and stand strong in the storm.

God's Word is our most valuable posses-sion, and its unfolding gives light in the darkest places. It directs us to wisdom, lifts our burdens, brings joy, guides our steps, and leads to salva-tion. Time and time again, it has proven to be our rescue from life's strife. How do we reap the benefits of God's Word? Study it!

In this 100-day devotional are 100 uplifting scriptures for you to study. In just a few minutes a day, you will reap the eternal treasures waiting for those who please God. Each scripture is your daily bread to digest and be nurtured. With these scriptures, short prayers, and snippets of encouragement, you will find direction for effective, day-to-day living.

The goal is to establish a consistent study habit that causes you to grow in wisdom and favor with God and man as you act justly, love mercy, and walk humbly with God.

Let's Stay Connected

Connect with Us: eddiejames.com

Connect with Us: dreamlifecenters.com

Find/Follow Us: Instagram: eddiejames_

Find/Follow Us: Facebook: Eddie James (Official)

Find/Follow Us: Twitter: ejworship

Watch Us: eddiejames.tv

Download Us: freshwinemusic.com

Pray 4 Us: In Jesus Name

Day 1

MORE THAN ENOUGH!

> *Jesus answered, "The foremost is, 'Hear, O Israel! The Lord our God is one Lord. (Mark 12:29)*

There's only one true and living God. He's more than enough!

_____

_____

_____

_____

_____

_____

_____

_____

_____

_____

Day 2

GIVE HIM ALL

> *And you shall love the Lord your God with all your heart, and with all your soul, and with all your mind, and with all your strength.*
>
> (Mark 12:30)

Don't hold anything back! Give Jesus 100% of your capacity to love. You're safe with Him.

_____

_____

_____

_____

_____

_____

_____

_____

Day 3

FILLED WITH HEAVEN'S BEST

> *The second is this, 'You shall love your neighbor as yourself.' There is no other commandment greater than these.* (Mark 12:31)

Love yourself by filling up with all heaven has to give us. Then pour into others what you have been freely given by grace.

_____

_____

_____

_____

_____

_____

_____

Day 4

SPEAK LIFE

> *If I speak with the tongues of men and of angels, but do not have love, I have become a noisy gong or a clanging cymbal.*
>
> (1 Corinthians 13:1)

The same mouth God gives grace to speak in a different language, is the very mouth He will use to speak life to others in the language you understand.

_____

_____

_____

_____

_____

Day 5

LOVE OR NOTHING

> *If I have the gift of prophecy, and know all mysteries and all knowledge; and if I have all faith, so as to remove mountains, but do not have love, I am nothing.*
>
> (1 Corinthians 13:2)

Love should always motivate the gift in which you operate.

_____

_____

_____

_____

_____

_____

Day 6

SELFIE SACRIFICES

And if I give all my possessions to feed the poor, and if I surrender my body to be burned, but do not have love, it profits me nothing.

(1 Corinthians 12:3)

Great acts of sacrifices not motivated by love are like posing for a selfie. You're simply trying to look good in front of other people.

_____

_____

_____

_____

_____

_____

Day 7

SWEET LOVE

> *Love is patient, love is kind and is not jealous; love does not brag and is not arrogant.*
>
> (1 Corinthians 13:4)

Notice it didn't say, "Love is chocolates, flowers, movies, and sex."

_____

_____

_____

_____

_____

_____

_____

_____

_____

Day 8

BE HEALED

> Love does not act unbecomingly; it does not seek its own, is not provoked, does not take into account a wrong suffered.
>
> (1 Corinthians 13:5)

If you tend to be clingy, needy, and have used people to medicate your brokenness, I declare healing over you. In Jesus' name.

_____

_____

_____

_____

_____

Day 9

TRUE LOVE

> *Love does not rejoice in unright-eousness, but rejoices with the truth.* (1 Corinthians 13:6)

You know you are growing in love when you long for truth, even if it hurts.

_____

_____

_____

_____

_____

_____

_____

_____

_____

Day 10

STUBBORN LOVE

> *Love bears all things, believes all things, hopes all things, endures all things.* (1 Corinthians 13:7)

Love doesn't quit. Love doesn't give up. Love doesn't throw in the towel.

_____

_____

_____

_____

_____

_____

_____

_____

_____

Day 11

PERPETUAL LOVE

> *Love never fails; but if there are gifts of prophecy, they will be done away; if there are tongues, they will cease; if there is knowledge, it will be done away.*
>
> (1 Corinthians 13:8)

Spiritual gifts are temporal; love lasts forever.

_____

_____

_____

_____

_____

_____

_____

_____

Day 12

A Little Bit at a Time

> For we know in part and we prophesy in part.
>
> (1 Corinthians 13:9)

Remember, you don't know everything. When God speaks to us, He reveals what we need a piece at a time.

_____

_____

_____

_____

_____

_____

_____

_____

Day 13

DIVINE ESCORTS

> *But when the perfect comes, the partial will be done away.*
>
> (1 Corinthians 13:10)

Spiritual gifts such as prophecy are God's divine escorts that take you to the place of love. Once you get to love, which is perfect, the escorts are no longer necessary.

_____
_____
_____
_____
_____
_____
_____
_____

Day 14

TIME TO MATURE

> *When I was a child, I used to speak like a child, think like a child, reason like a child; when I became a man, I did away with childish things.* (1 Corinthians 13:11)

Today, I choose to mature in love.

_____

_____

_____

_____

_____

_____

_____

_____

_____

Day 15

MORE REVELATION

> For now we see in a mirror dimly, but then face to face; now I know in part, but then I will know fully just as I also have been fully known. (1 Corinthians 13:12)

Father, increase my revelation of Jesus, thus, increasing my revelation of love.

_____

_____

_____

_____

_____

_____

_____

Day 16

LOVE IS THE BOSS

> *But now faith, hope, love, abide these three; but the 1greatest of these is love.* (1 Corinthians 13:13)

Lord, let faith, hope, and love abide in me, but let love take up the most room in my heart.

_____

_____

_____

_____

_____

_____

_____

_____

Day 17

Closer, Lord

When Jesus saw the crowds, He went up on the mountain; and after He sat down, His disciples came to Him. (Matthew 5:1)

Lord, draw me closer to You.

_____

_____

_____

_____

_____

_____

_____

_____

_____

Day 18

Teach Me

> He opened His mouth and began
> to teach them, saying.
>
> (Matthew 5:2)

Lord, open my ears to hear You; open my
heart that it may be teachable.

_____

_____

_____

_____

_____

_____

_____

_____

_____

_____

Day 19

NEEDY

> *Blessed are the poor in spirit, for theirs is the kingdom of heaven.*
>
> (Matthew 5:3)

Lord, help me to recognize that I need You.

_____

_____

_____

_____

_____

_____

_____

_____

_____

_____

Day 20

LORD OF THE BROKEN

> *Blessed are those who mourn, for they shall be comforted.*
> (Matthew 5:4)

Thank You, Lord, for being drawn to the broken and weeping with the downtrodden.

_____

_____

_____

_____

_____

_____

_____

_____

_____

Day 21

BLESSINGS OF THE GENTLE

Blessed are the gentle, for they shall inherit the earth.

(Matthew 5:5)

Lord, give me a spirit of gentleness that I may be a wise steward of the inheritance received from You in this life.

_____

_____

_____

_____

_____

_____

_____

_____

Day 22

HUNGRY FOR GOODNESS

> *Blessed are those who hunger and thirst for righteousness, for they shall be satisfied.* (Matthew 5:6)

Lord, give me an appetite for being in right standing with You.

_____

_____

_____

_____

_____

_____

_____

_____

_____

Day 23

MERCY FOR MERCY

> *Blessed are the merciful, for they shall receive mercy. (Matthew 5:7)*

May I never hold a grudge or be unforgiving.

_____

_____

_____

_____

_____

_____

_____

_____

_____

_____

Day 24

SEARCH AND PURGE

> *Blessed are the pure in heart, for they shall see God.* (Matthew 5:8)

Lord, search my heart. Remove lusts, motives, and intentions that are not of You.

_____

_____

_____

_____

_____

_____

_____

_____

_____

_____

_____

Day 25

BLESSED PEACE

> Blessed are the peacemakers, for
> they shall be called sons of God.
> (Matthew 5:9)

Lord, teach me to seek, walk in, and main-
tain peace at all times.

_____

_____

_____

_____

_____

_____

_____

_____

_____

_____

Day 26

I'm Blessed!

> *Blessed are those who have been persecuted for the sake of right-eousness, for theirs is the king-dom of heaven.* (Matthew 5:10)

Lord, when I face the day of persecution, may my perspective be that "I'm still blessed."

_____
_____
_____
_____
_____
_____
_____
_____

Day 27

HATED BUT BLESSED

> *Blessed are you when people insult you and persecute you, and falsely say all kinds of evil against you because of Me. (Matthew 5:11)*

If my love for You brings haters, may I see myself as blessed.

_____

_____

_____

_____

_____

_____

_____

_____

Day 28

GLADLY PERSECUTED

> *Rejoice and be glad, for your reward in heaven is great; for in the same way they persecuted the prophets who were before you.*
>
> (Matthew 5:12)

Lord, help me to rejoice when insulted and be glad when persecuted for Jesus. I know my reward is in heaven.

_____

_____

_____

_____

_____

_____

SAVORY SALT

> *You are the salt of the earth; but if the salt has become tasteless, how can it be made salty again? It is no longer good for anything, except to be thrown out and trampled under foot by men.*
>
> (Matthew 5:13)

Lord, help me to walk in my purpose and make a difference in this world.

_____

_____

_____

_____

_____

Day 30

LIGHT IN DARKNESS

> *You are the light of the world. A city set on a hill cannot be hidden.*
> (Matthew 5:14)

Lord, let Your light of truth cause me to shine bright in dark times.

_____

_____

_____

_____

_____

_____

_____

_____

Day 31

PUT ME ON THE LAMPSTAND

> *Nor does anyone light a lamp and put it under a basket, but on the lampstand, and it gives light to all who are in the house.*
>
> (Matthew 5:15)

Lord, place me where the light You put in me can have the most impact.

_____

_____

_____

_____

_____

_____

_____

_____

Day 32

A LIGHT OF GLORY

> Let your light shine before men in such a way that they may see your good works, and glorify your Father who is in heaven.
>
> (Matthew 5:16)

Lord, may everything I say and do bring glory to You.

_____

_____

_____

_____

_____

_____

_____

Day 33

EMPOWERING GRACE

> *Do not think that I came to abolish the Law or the Prophets; I did not come to abolish but to fulfill.*
>
> (Matthew 5:17)

Grace is not an excuse to sin but empowerment to reflect the nature of Jesus.

_____

_____

_____

_____

_____

_____

_____

_____

_____

My Everyday Reflection

> *For truly I say to you, until heaven and earth pass away, not the smallest letter or stroke shall pass from the Law until all is accomplished.* (Matthew 5:18)

Lord, I love and embrace the principles of Your Word. May my life be a reflection of it.

_____

_____

_____

_____

_____

_____

_____

_____

Day 35

No to Hypocrisy

> For I say to you that unless your righteousness surpasses that of the scribes and Pharisees, you will not enter the kingdom of heaven.
>
> (Matthew 5:20)

Lord, I don't want to say one thing in public and do something else behind closed doors. I want my actions and heart's position to be real and genuine.

_____

_____

_____

_____

_____

Day 36

Free Heart

> *You have heard that the ancients were told, 'You shall not commit murder' and 'Whoever commits murder shall be liable to the court.'* (Matthew 5:21)

Lord, Your Word teaches us not to kill. Take out any seeds planted in my heart that would put that desire in me. I want a heart that is free when I stand before the righteous judge in the heavenly court.

_____

_____

_____

_____

Day 37

CONQUER ANGER

> *But I say to you that everyone who is angry with his brother shall be guilty before the court; and whoever says to his brother, 'You good-for-nothing,' shall be guilty before the supreme court; and whoever says, 'You fool,' shall be guilty enough to go into the fiery hell.* (Matthew 5:22)

Lord, keep me from the spirit of anger. Help me to watch what I say in challenging moments. May I look to You for peace and grace to respond as You desire.

HEALTHY RELATIONSHIPS

> *Therefore if you are presenting your offering at the altar, and there remember that your brother has something against you, leave your offering there before the altar and go; first be reconciled to your brother, and then come and present your offering.*
>
> (Matthew 5:23)

Lord, I want to have healthy relationships at all times. Teach me how to gracefully work through differences and reconcile quickly, so I'm always free to worship and honor You.

FAVOR IN LEGAL BATTLES

Make friends quickly with your opponent at law while you are with him on the way, so that your opponent may not hand you over to the judge, and the judge to the officer, and you be thrown into prison. (Matthew 5:25)

Lord, I never want to be in a legal battle. Should the day come, give me favor with those who oppose me. May every legal battle be settled in a way that glorifies You.

_____

_____

_____

Day 40

MY MOMENT IN COURT

Truly I say to you, you will not come out of there until you have paid up the last cent.

(Matthew 5:26)

Lord, I pray that my actions and lifestyle choices are of such honor and integrity that favor and grace are released should I ever have a moment in court.

_____

_____

_____

_____

_____

_____

Day 41

FAITHFUL ALWAYS

> *You have heard that it was said,*
> *'You shall not commit adultery.'*
> (Matthew 5:27)

Lord, teach me to be faithful in every way, even as You are faithful.

_____

_____

_____

_____

_____

_____

_____

_____

_____

Day 42

Purity, Not Pornography

> But I say to you that everyone who looks at a woman with lust for her has already committed adultery with her in his heart.
>
> (Matthew 5:28)

Lord, keep my eyes and my heart pure. Let me hate and stay away from pornography and other perversions.

_____

_____

_____

_____

_____

Day 43

TEMPTATION
BE GONE!

> *If your right eye makes you stumble, tear it out and throw it from you; for it is better for you to lose one of the parts of your body, than for your whole body to be thrown into hell.* (Matthew 5:29)

Lord, I choose to remove every possible temptation from my life. Nothing I have is worth my relationship with You.

_____

_____

_____

_____

LIFE AND DEATH CHOICES

> *If your right hand makes you stumble, cut it off and throw it from you; for it is better for you to lose one of the parts of your body, than for your whole body to go into hell.* (Matthew 5:30)

Lord, I choose to surround myself with people who help me do the right things. May my life choices always reflect Your Word and will.

_____

_____

_____

_____

Day 45

THE DIRTY D-WORD

It was said, 'Whoever sends his wife away, let him give her a certificate of divorce. (Matthew 5:31)

Lord, You hate divorce (Malachi 2:16). Keep it as far away from me as possible.

_____

_____

_____

_____

_____

_____

_____

_____

_____

FAITHFUL IN MARRIAGE

> *But I say to you that everyone who divorces his wife, except for the reason of unchastity, makes her commit adultery; and whoever marries a divorced woman commits adultery.* (Matthew 5:32)

Lord, faithfulness is Your heart. May the marriage You give me be built on the foundation of Your love.

_____

_____

_____

_____

_____

Day 47

MY WORD, MY BOND

Again, you have heard that the ancients were told, 'You shall not make false vows, but shall fulfill your vows to the Lord.

(Matthew 5:33)

Lord, let me be a person of integrity who keeps their word.

_____

_____

_____

_____

_____

_____

_____

Day 48

SWEAR NOT!

> *But I say to you, make no oath at all, either by heaven, for it is the throne of God.* (Matthew 5:34)

Saying words like "I swear to God" should *never* come out of my mouth.

_____

_____

_____

_____

_____

_____

_____

_____

_____

Day 49

COMMITMENT COSTS

*Or by the earth, for it is the foot-
stool of His feet, or by Jerusalem,
for it is the city of the great King.*
(Matthew 5:35)

Lord, teach me to count the cost of the commitments I make, so I don't ever break them.

_____

_____

_____

_____

_____

_____

_____

_____

_____

Day 50

"I Will" Is Enough

> Nor shall you make an oath by your head, for you cannot make one hair white or black.
>
> (Matthew 5:36)

Lord, teach me not to say, "I swear to..." to convince someone I'm telling the truth.

_____

_____

_____

_____

_____

_____

_____

_____

Day 51

YES OR NO

> But let your statement be, 'Yes, yes' or 'No, no'; anything beyond these is of evil. (Matthew 5:37)

Lord, if I say it, that should settle it. Help me to live like this.

_____

_____

_____

_____

_____

_____

_____

_____

_____

Day 52

VENGEANCE IS
NOT MINE

> *You have heard that it was said, 'An eye for an eye, and a tooth for a tooth.* (Matthew 5:38)

Lord, retaliation is never Your heart. May it never be mine.

_____

_____

_____

_____

_____

_____

_____

_____

_____

Day 53

TURN THE
OTHER CHEEK

> *But I say to you, do not resist an evil person; but whoever slaps you on your right cheek, turn the other to him also. (Matthew 5:39)*

Lord, may Your love and nature shine in me when I am mistreated.

_____

_____

_____

_____

_____

_____

_____

_____

Day 54

BLESS YOUR HATERS

> *If anyone wants to sue you and take your shirt, let him have your coat also.* (Matthew 5:40)

Lord, give me a heart to bless those who don't mean well for me.

_____

_____

_____

_____

_____

_____

_____

_____

_____

Day 55

GRACE FOR THE EXTRA MILE

Whoever forces you to go one mile, go with him two. (Matthew 5:41)

Lord, I thank You for grace to go the extra mile, even when I don't want to.

_____

_____

_____

_____

_____

_____

_____

_____

_____

_____

Day 56

CHOOSING TO GIVE

Give to him who asks of you, and do not turn away from him who wants to borrow from you.

(Matthew 5:42)

Lord, I choose to be a giver.

_____

_____

_____

_____

_____

_____

_____

_____

_____

Day 57

A HATER'S FOLLY

> You have heard that it was said,
> 'You shall love your neighbor and
> hate your enemy.' (Matthew 5:43)

Hate destroys the hater, not the one hated.

_____

_____

_____

_____

_____

_____

_____

_____

_____

Day 58

LOVER OF MY ENEMIES

> *But I say to you, love your enemies and pray for those who persecute you. (Matthew 5:44)*

Make me an intercessor for my enemies and persecutors. Show me how to love them.

_____

_____

_____

_____

_____

_____

_____

_____

_____

_____

Day 59

GOD'S DNA CARRIER

> So that you may be sons of your Father who is in heaven; for He causes His sun to rise on the evil and the good, and sends rain on the righteous and the unrighteous. (Matthew 5:45)

I am Your child. I carry Your DNA. Your love is unconditional. As the sun and rain release themselves without regard to the character of those who benefit from them, may I love the same way.

_____

_____

_____

Day 60

LOVE UNUSUAL

> *For if you love those who love you, what reward do you have? Do not even the tax collectors do the same?* (Matthew 5:46)

Loving others who love you is done by the worst of sinners. It's great to do that. However, that alone doesn't reflect the nature of Jesus.

_____

_____

_____

_____

_____

_____

Day 61

COURAGEOUSLY LOVING

> *If you greet only your brothers, what more are you doing than others? Do not even the Gentiles do the same? (Matthew 5:47)*

Speaking to those you already have relationships with is normal. Non-Christians do this all the time. Lord, help me to be courageously loving to those who hate me and to those I've never met.

_____

_____

_____

_____

_____

PERFECT LIKE YOUR FATHER

> *Therefore you are to be perfect,*
> *as your heavenly Father is perfect.*
> (Matthew 5:48)

Lord, I understand "perfect" means complete, whole, to come into fullness and maturity. Help me to grow and mature that I may be the son You created me to be.

NO LONGER A MAN-PLEASER

> *Beware of practicing your righteousness before men to be noticed by them; otherwise you have no reward with your Father who is in heaven.* (Matthew 6:1)

Lord, free me from craving the applause of man. May I seek to honor You alone.

_____

_____

_____

_____

_____

_____

Day 64

LORD, "LIKE" ME

> *So when you give to the poor, do not sound a trumpet before you, as the hypocrites do in the synagogues and in the streets, so that they may be honored by men. Truly I say to you, they have their reward in full.* (Matthew 6:2)

Lord, may the good I do not be for selfies, Snapchat, and Instagram posts. May the only likes I'm after be Yours.

_____

_____

_____

_____

Day 65

SECRET SERVICE

> *But when you give to the poor, do not let your left hand know what your right hand is doing.*
>
> (Matthew 6:3)

Teach me to serve people without letting others know about it.

_____

_____

_____

_____

_____

_____

_____

_____

Day 66

GOD SEES YOUR GOOD DEEDS

> *So that your giving will be in se-cret; and your Father who sees what is done in secret will reward you. (Matthew 6:4)*

Lord, thank You for never missing the good I do. You take notice of everything, and it moves Your heart. That's all I care about.

_____

_____

_____

_____

_____

_____

Day 67

GOD-PLEASING PRAYERS

> *So do not be like them; for your Father knows what you need before you ask Him.*
>
> (Matthew 6:8)

Teach me to pray in a way that pleases You. After all, I'm talking to You. I want the words I say to You to come from my heart and be pleasing to You.

_____

_____

_____

_____

_____

Day 68

THE SECRET PLACE

> *But you, when you pray, go into your inner room, close your door and pray to your Father who is in secret, and your Father who sees what is done in secret will reward you.* (Matthew 6:6)

Thank You, Lord, for the "Secret Place." May this place be what I treasure the most about our relationship.

_____

_____

_____

_____

_____

Day 69

HEART TALK

And when you are praying, do not use meaningless repetition as the Gentiles do, for they suppose that they will be heard for their many words. (Matthew 6:7)

Lord, I want to speak to You from my heart, not just from what I heard other people say.

_____

_____

_____

_____

_____

_____

_____

Day 70

STRENGTH IN PRIVATE

> *When you pray, you are not to be like the hypocrites; for they love to stand and pray in the synagogues and on the street corners so that they may be seen by men. Truly I say to you, they have their reward in full.* (Matthew 6:5)

Lord, strengthen my private prayer life.

_____

_____

_____

_____

_____

_____

Day 71

HIS SACRED NAME

> *Pray, then, in this way: 'Our Father who is in heaven, Hallowed be Your name.* (Matthew 6:9)

Thank You that I'm your child. I hold Your name sacred and holy in my heart.

_____

_____

_____

_____

_____

_____

_____

_____

_____

Day 72

MAKE EARTH A REFLECTION OF HEAVEN

Your kingdom come. Your will be done, on earth as it is in heaven.
(Matthew 6:10)

Lord, may my prayers agree with Your heart, so the earth would look like heaven.

_____

_____

_____

_____

_____

_____

_____

_____

Day 73

DELIVER ME FROM COMPROMISE

> *And do not lead us into temptation, but deliver us from evil. For Yours is the kingdom and the power and the glory forever. Amen.* (Matthew 6:13)

Lord, help me to never find myself in a place of compromise. If I am ever there, deliver me. May I honor You in worship, for the kingdom, power, and glory are forever Yours.

_____

_____

_____

_____

Day 74

FORGIVEN TO FORGIVE

> *And forgive us our debts, as we also have forgiven our debtors.*
>
> (Matthew 6:12)

Lord, teach me to forgive because I need to be forgiven. Help me keep this as a part of my daily requests from You.

_____

_____

_____

_____

_____

_____

_____

_____

_____

Day 75

FED BY THE WORD

Give us this day our daily bread.
(Matthew 6:11)

Lord, may my daily prayer be that I am daily fed Your Word.

_____

_____

_____

_____

_____

_____

_____

_____

_____

_____

Day 76

NO OFFENSE

For if you forgive others for their transgressions, your heavenly Father will also forgive you.

(Matthew 6:14)

Lord, purify my heart. Remove resentment, bitterness, and grudges against anyone, so I may receive forgiveness when I need it.

_____

_____

_____

_____

_____

_____

_____

Day 77

YES TO FORGIVENESS

> *But if you do not forgive others,*
> *then your Father will not forgive*
> *your transgressions.*
> (Matthew 6:15)

Lord, when I don't forgive others, I hinder my forgiveness. So I say "yes" to forgiveness, even when I don't feel it.

_____

_____

_____

_____

_____

_____

_____

_____

APPROVED BY GOD

> *Whenever you fast, do not put on a gloomy face as the hypocrites do, for they neglect their appearance so that they will be noticed by men when they are fasting. Truly I say to you, they have their reward in full.* (Matthew 6:16)

Lord, deliver me from needing and seeking man's approval.

_____

_____

_____

_____

_____

Day 79

Unknown Consecration

> But you, when you fast, anoint
> your head and wash your face.
>
> (Matthew 6:17)

Lord, I want my life of consecration to be so personal that people will never know when I'm doing it.

_____

_____

_____

_____

_____

_____

_____

_____

_____

Day 80

IT'S ALL ABOUT YOU

> *So that your fasting will not be noticed by men, but by your Father who is in secret; and your Father who sees what is done in secret will reward you.* (Matthew 6:18)

Lord, my life of devotion is all about You—no one else.

_____

_____

_____

_____

_____

_____

_____

_____

Day 81

NOT OF THIS WORLD

> *Do not store up for yourselves treasures on earth, where moth and rust destroy, and where thieves break in and steal.*
>
> (Matthew 6:19)

Lord, help me not to make life about the things of this world.

_____

_____

_____

_____

_____

_____

_____

_____

INDESTRUCTIBLE TREASURES

> *But store up for yourselves treasures in heaven, where neither moth nor rust destroys, and where thieves do not break in or steal* (Matthew 6:20)

Lord, I want heavenly treasures: wisdom, honor, holiness, peace, and love. No one can ever steal these treasures, and they will never be destroyed.

_____

_____

_____

_____

_____

Day 83

ETERNAL TREASURES

> *For where your treasure is, there your heart will be also.*
>
> (Matthew 6:21)

Lord, I choose to set my heart on the things that are eternal. Thank You for all the blessings in this life. I will use them to advance Your kingdom in this world. My treasure is in heaven. That's where my heart is.

_____

_____

_____

_____

_____

_____

IN HEAVEN'S EYES

> *Do not judge so that you will not be judged.* (Matthew 7:1)

Lord, teach me to see people the way You see them when they are at their weakest.

_____

_____

_____

_____

_____

_____

_____

_____

_____

_____

Day 85

JUDGE AND BE JUDGED

> *For in the way you judge, you will be judged; and by your standard of measure, it will be measured to you.* (Matthew 7:2)

I realize when I am critical of others, I am asking for that same measure and standard to be placed on me.

_____

_____

_____

_____

_____

_____

_____

_____

Day 86

A LOOK AT SELF

> *Why do you look at the speck that is in your brother's eye, but do not notice the log that is in your own eye?* (Matthew 7:3)

Lord, help me to always work on my weaknesses and not highlight the weaknesses of others.

_____

_____

_____

_____

_____

_____

_____

Day 87

WORK ON THE LOG

> Or how can you say to your brother, 'Let me take the speck out of your eye,' and behold, the log is in your own eye? (Matthew 7:4)

Lord, if I'm ever in conflict with my brother, help me to stop, recognize, admit, and change the wrongs I've brought into the conflict.

_____

_____

_____

_____

_____

_____

_____

Day 88

THE ROAD LESS TRAVELED

> *For the gate is small and the way is narrow that leads to life, and there are few who find it.*
>
> (Matthew 7:14)

Lord, give me grace to say yes to the narrow way. May I be OK with walking alone or only with a few.

_____

_____

_____

_____

_____

_____

_____

Don't Cast Your Pearls to Swine

> *Do not give what is holy to dogs, and do not throw your pearls before swine, or they will trample them under their feet, and turn and tear you to pieces.*
>
> (Matthew 7:6)

Lord, You have given me treasure. What I have is holy and more valuable than pearls. You have blessed me with purpose and a future. Protect me from connecting with people whose characters are like dogs and swine. Help me have healthy relationships and connect with the right people who will bring out the best in me.

Day 90

COURAGE TO PURSUE

*Ask, and it will be given to you;
seek, and you will find; knock,
and it will be opened to you.*

(Matthew 7:7)

Lord, increase my courage and faith to pursue You and the doors You call me to. May I walk in Your will and Your way.

_____

_____

_____

_____

_____

_____

_____

Day 91

PROMISES RECEIVED

> *For everyone who asks receives, and he who seeks finds, and to him who knocks it will be opened.*
> (Matthew 7:8)

Thank You, Lord, for the promises in Your Word. When I ask, seek, and knock according to Your will, I am sure to receive. Hallelujah!

_____

_____

_____

_____

_____

_____

Day 92

GOOD, GOOD FATHER

> *Or what man is there among you who, when his son asks for a loaf, will give him a stone?*
>
> (Matthew 7:9)

God, thank You for being such a good Father.

_____

_____

_____

_____

_____

_____

_____

_____

_____

Day 93

TRUSTWORTHY FATHER

Or if he asks for a fish, he will not give him a snake, will he?

(Matthew 7:10)

Lord, You are trustworthy. We have the confidence You will not deceive or abuse us.

_____

_____

_____

_____

_____

_____

_____

_____

_____

Day 94

So Good!

> If you then, being evil, know how
> to give good gifts to your children,
> how much more will your Father
> who is in heaven give what is
> good to those who ask Him!
>
> (Matthew 7:11)

Praise You, Father, for being so good to us.

_____

_____

_____

_____

_____

_____

_____

_____

Day 95

GOD'S GOLDEN RULE

> *In everything, therefore, treat*
> *people the same way you want*
> *them to treat you, for this is the*
> *Law and the Prophets.*
> (Matthew 7:12)

Lord, this is the golden rule of Your Word. Help me to live by this and walk it out every day with everyone I come in contact with.

_____

_____

_____

_____

_____

_____

WALKING THE WALK

> *Enter through the narrow gate;*
> *for the gate is wide and the way*
> *is broad that leads to destruction,*
> *and there are many who enter*
> *through it. (Matthew 7:13)*

Lord, Your principles may seem strict. Give me grace to say "no" to what appears easy, popular, and the road most people travel.

_____

_____

_____

_____

_____

Day 97

CLEAR VISION

> *You hypocrite, first take the log out of your own eye, and then you will see clearly to take the speck out of your brother's eye.* (Matthew 7:5)

Lord, help me to humble myself in relationships. Sometimes You allow conflict so that I can take my eyes off my brother's weaknesses and focus on my own issues.

_____

_____

_____

_____

_____

_____

Day 98

EARS TO HEAR

> *Therefore everyone who hears these words of Mine and acts on them, may be compared to a wise man who built his house on the rock.* (Matthew 7:24)

Lord, give me ears to hear and obey Your Word as I build this house called "life."

_____

_____

_____

_____

_____

_____

_____

_____

Day 99

SOLID ROCK

And the rain fell, and the floods came, and the winds blew and slammed against that house; and yet it did not fall, for it had been founded on the rock.

(Matthew 7:25)

Lord, Your Word is the foundation my life is built on. So I know I will remain standing no matter how difficult the storm may be.

_____

_____

_____

_____

_____

Day 100

I'm No Fool

> *Everyone who hears these words of Mine and does not act on them, will be like a foolish man who built his house on the sand. The rain fell, and the floods came, and the winds blew and slammed against that house; and it fell—and great was its fall.*
>
> (Matthew 7:26-27)

Lord, I declare that I will be wise and not foolish. My life will not fall but remain standing through every storm I face because I've surrendered to You and Your Word every day. In Jesus' name. Amen.

About the Author

Eddie James is a worship artist, minister, and founder of Eddie James Ministries, Eddie James Productions, DreamLife, Fresh Wine Records, and Fresh Wine Publishing. He has been in ministry for more than 30 years and traveled full time for 18 years.

As an internationally renowned worship artist, he releases his songs of worship to many of the world's most impactful ministries. These ministries include Daniel Kolenda, Bishop T.D. Jakes, Lou Engle, The Call, Bill Johnson, Bethel Music, Perry Stone, Karen Wheaton, Kirk Franklin, and many more. His song writing, production, and artistry have carried his music to the top of the Billboard Charts. "I Am," "Lord, You're Holy," "Psalm 23," "You've Been So Faithful," "Breakthrough," and "Freedom" are just a few of the songs for which he is known.

His songs have been performed by a wide range of music artists and ministries, from

Judy Jacobs, Karen Wheaton and Helen Baylor to Lakeland Church, Brooklyn Tabernacle, Mississippi Mass Choir. His works have been featured on Fox News, Glen Beck, Oprah Winfrey Network and "Lion of Judah" produced by Warner Brothers. His music and sound are sought around the world, evidenced by his appearances on TBN, God-TV, Daystar, "Sid Roth's It's Supernatural" and in magazines like "Charisma."

Eddie rescues, restores, and raises high school and college-age youth who are coming out of drug addiction, street life, gangs, violence, abuse, and perverse lifestyles through a recovery program known as Dream-Life Ministries. When he is not traveling, he is with his spiritual and adopted sons and daughters, teaching his discipleship program called "Discipleship N Arts" (DNA). Hundreds of youths have been empowered to experience a life of freedom and discover their true significance. Many of them now have ministries of their own or are serving in powerful ministries and churches.

Let's Stay Connected

Connect with Us: eddiejames.com

Connect with Us: dreamlifecenters.com

Find/Follow Us: Instagram: eddiejames_

Find/Follow Us: Facebook: Eddie James (Official)

Find/Follow Us: Twitter: ejworship

Watch Us: eddiejames.tv

Download Us: freshwinemusic.com

Pray 4 Us: In Jesus Name

www.ingramcontent.com/pod-product-compliance
Lightning Source LLC
Chambersburg PA
CBHW062004040426
42447CB00010B/1909